# The KIDS' YOGA BOOK of FEELINGS

by **Mary Humphrey**

Photos by
**Michael Frost**

Illustrations by
**Janet Hamlin**

Marshall Cavendish Children

# Introduction

## THE YOU INSIDE OF YOU

Feelings get trapped inside your body like words hidden in the pages of a closed book. Until the book is opened, no one can read what's there. In the same way, breathing deeply and moving your body in different positions, or poses, while doing yoga releases feelings that are caught inside your body. Yoga allows you to meet the you inside of you.

Each of the yoga poses in this book has an animal or familiar object linked to the feeling it expresses. Just as a butterfly is light and airy, the butterfly pose expresses joy and freedom. In contrast, the lion pose helps you let go of anger as you take a deep breath and roar. Some of the poses can be done with a friend, or you can enjoy doing yoga by yourself.

## WHAT IS YOGA?

The practice of yoga began in India more than five thousand years ago. It is an art that emphasizes healthy living and a calm, happy state of being. For thousands of years yogis, or wise teachers, taught yoga, and their teaching was passed from generation to generation. Then, about two thousand years ago, a teacher named Patanjali wrote down the practices and beliefs of yoga. This enabled even more people to learn about it. The word *yoga* means union. When doing the poses, the body, mind, and breath are brought together as a unit to create feelings of stability, calmness, and harmony.

## WHO CAN DO YOGA?

Anyone! Yoga is a non-competitive practice. Just as we all have different bodies, personalities, and interests, we can perform poses in our own unique ways. There is no absolutely correct style in which to do a pose.

# WHY DO YOGA?

Yoga is fun. Yoga keeps the body fit and flexible. The poses allow you to build strength and balance, and they help you to improve concentration as well. As you focus on each pose, your mind becomes calm and relaxed, allowing the feelings trapped inside you to be released.

# GETTING READY

Find a comfy, quiet place to practice in. Wear comfortable loose clothing or leotards that will allow you to move easily. Use props that make the exercises safe and easy to do. Yoga mats, sometimes called sticky mats, are designed to help you stand or balance firmly without slipping. Blocks, straps, and even a blanket can also aid you in the poses.

# AFFIRMATION

Each pose has a saying—called an affirmation—to go with it. The affirmation is the feeling released by the pose. The affirmation also sets an intention for your practice. It helps to bring about the harmony and feelings you want to experience while doing yoga. When you are in the pose, say the affirmation to yourself or out loud.

# BREATHING

Breathing is an important part of yoga. When done properly, breathing allows you to perform each pose more easily and helps create focus and balance. As you inhale, you breathe in oxygen and, as you exhale, you release carbon dioxide. Good breathing helps you to move into the pose and feel like the animal or object connected with it.

As you do your poses, breathe in slowly through your nose, inhaling full, deep breaths before letting go. This helps your body take in more oxygen and cleans out and exercises your lungs. Deep breathing also fills your whole body with oxygen and helps you to relax. After each pose, you should breathe in and out normally, as you relax.

# Lotus Blossom

## FEELING

# PEACEFUL

In the morning, when your body is just waking up, you can become the lotus blossom resting in the pond as it waits for the day to begin. Sit in a comfortable cross-legged pose and breathe quietly. Close your eyes and feel your breath as you inhale through your nose. Be aware of your body's sensations. Are you energetic, ready to move? Or are you feeling sleepy, slow to wake up? Listen to your body. Pay attention to your feelings and sensations and calmly let them go.

## AFFIRMATION

# I feel calm and steady, ready to start the day.

As you become the lotus blossom, breathe in and out ten times.

# Butterfly

## FEELING

# JOY

As you begin to feel livelier, uncross your legs and bring the soles of your feet together and in close to your body. Clasp your hands around your ankles and open your knees out to both sides. Stretch your spine to the sky and flop your legs up and down like butterfly wings.

## AFFIRMATION

# I feel carefree and joyful.

As your butterfly lands, let your knees fall toward the floor and relax them above or on the floor.

As you become the butterfly, breathe in and out five times.

# Mountain

## FEELING

# CONNECTION

Come to a standing position and drop your arms to your sides with your feet close together. Roll from the balls of your feet to the heels and back again until you are stable and rooted. Stand straight and tall. Lift your head to the sky while gazing straight ahead, and feel your feet touch the earth just like a mountain that stands strong and tall.

## AFFIRMATION

## I feel connected to both the earth and the sky.

As you become the mountain, breathe in and out five times.

# Tree

## FEELING
## BEING CENTERED

Focus on your right leg and imagine that roots are growing from the bottom of your foot into the ground. Press your foot solidly to the mat. Rest the sole of your left foot on the inside of your right leg and try to balance. Focus on a distant object as you move your left leg higher and rest it comfortably on your right inner thigh. You may bring your hands together in a prayer position in front of your chest. Maintain your focus and stability by breathing deeply.

## AFFIRMATION
## I feel centered when I am rooted to the ground.

As you become the tree, breathe in and out five times.

When you have finished balancing on the right side, repeat the same pose on the left leg till you feel you have achieved balance on both sides of your body.

# Elephant

## FEELINGS

## CURIOSITY, EXCITEMENT

Bend forward so that your head and arms hang down. Look backward between your knees. Clasp your hands in front of your legs to form the elephant's trunk. Gently twist your trunk from side to side as if you are searching for peanuts.

## AFFIRMATION

## I feel curious and excited.

As you become the elephant, breathe in and out five times as you sway your trunk back and forth.

# Polar Bear

## FEELING

# STABILITY

Get down on your hands and knees. Place your hands beneath your shoulders and spread your fingers out like starfish. Make sure there is space between your knees. Lift your head and gaze straight ahead. You want to feel fully balanced and grounded just like the polar bear that stands firmly on a patch of ice.

## AFFIRMATION

# I feel balanced and grounded.

As you become the polar bear, breathe in and out five times.

# Down Dog
# Puppy Dog

## DOWN DOG AND PUPPY DOG FEELINGS

### PERKY AND HAPPY

Press your hands against the mat and lift your bottom high in the air. Spread your feet about hip-width apart. Let your head hang down and your heels fall toward the mat. Feel the strength in your arms and shoulders. You are now a happy dog ready to wag its tail. As you become the dog, breathe in and out five times.

### AFFIRMATION

I feel happy and perky.

### PUPPY DOG

To change from Down Dog to Puppy Dog, slide your arms forward and rest your elbows on the mat. Drop your knees to the mat and slide your bottom back to your heels. Wag your bottom as a puppy wags its tail.

### AFFIRMATION

I feel perky and ready to play.

As you become the puppy dog, breathe in and out five times.

# Cow ⚬ ⚬ Cat

## COW FEELINGS
## RELAXED AND CALM

Get down on all fours with your palms and knees firmly planted on the mat and your knees hip-width apart. Lift up your head and breathe in. Let your back sag just like a cow that is calm and content in a sunny meadow.

### AFFIRMATION
I feel relaxed and calm.

### CAT FEELINGS
### READY, ALERT

Breathe out and then arch and round your back like a cat that is alert, ready for anything to happen. Look back between your thighs and make sure there is space between your knees.

### AFFIRMATION
I am alert and ready for anything.

Go back and forth between the cow and the cat. Remember to breathe in as you become the cow and breathe out as you become the cat. Try this five times before moving on to the next pose.

# Mouse

## FEELING

# PEACEFUL

Sit on your knees and drop your head gently to the floor. Let your arms hang loosely by your sides with your forehead gently touching the mat. Place your hands, palms up, next to your feet. Close your eyes and breathe deeply.

## AFFIRMATION

# When I let go completely, I feel peaceful.

As you become the mouse, breathe in and out five times or more, completely relaxing and letting go.

# Lion

## FEELING

# RELEASING ANGER

To go from the mouse to the lion, come to a sitting position, resting on your heels. Place your hands on your thighs and lift your head. Breathe in deeply and lean forward. Stick your tongue out and roar like a lion, letting your anger go.

## AFFIRMATION

### When I feel anger, I let it go.

Sit back quietly on your heels and close your eyes. Try the lion several times before moving on to the next pose.

# Proud Warrior

## FEELINGS

## STRENGTH AND CONFIDENCE

Stand at the back of your mat. Take a giant step forward with your right foot. Turn your back foot out slightly and bend your right knee. Your hips should face forward like two headlights as you breathe in. With your palms facing each other, lift your hands up to the sky. Gaze upward.

## AFFIRMATION

## I feel strong and confident.

As you become the proud warrior, breathe in and out five times. When you finish, take a step back so that your right foot meets your left foot.

Try the same pose by switching feet. Move your left foot forward and keep your left leg bent.

Remember to say, "I feel strong and confident."

When you finish, step to the back of the mat before moving to the next pose.

# Bridge

## FEELINGS

## OPENNESS, ACCEPTANCE

Lie down on your back and place your feet hip-width apart. Bend your knees and bring your heels closer to your bottom. Breathe in deeply as you lift your bottom up as high as possible. Push your arms close together and clasp your hands. Feel strength in your legs as you continue to breathe.

## AFFIRMATION

## I feel open to all possibilities.

As you become the bridge, breathe in and out five times before gently lowering your back to the floor while you release your hands.

# Cobra

### FEELING

## COURAGE

Lie on your tummy with your forehead on the mat. Press your elbows to your sides and line up your hands beneath your shoulders. Breathe in deeply. Slowly raise your head and shoulders like a cobra. Straighten your arms and gaze around. Press your hands down and gaze ahead.

### AFFIRMATION

## I rise to meet all challenges.

Breathe in and out as you gently lower your body to the mat.

# Swan

## FEELING
## CONTENTMENT

Get down on your hands and knees. Think about the story of the ugly duckling who thought he was different. Then, remember how he became transformed into a swan. Lift your right arm and extend your hand straight ahead as you gaze forward. Then, extend your left leg back and flex your foot as you balance on your right knee.

## AFFIRMATION

# I understand and accept myself as I am.

Breathe in and out five times.

Try this on the other side, lifting your left hand as the swan's wing and balancing on your left knee with your right leg extended back.

# Dragon

## FEELINGS

# PASSION, CREATIVITY

Place your left knee on the mat and move your right foot forward about a foot. Take a deep breath in, lift your hands over your head, and then blow out fire like a dragon. Hold the pose for five dragon breaths.

## AFFIRMATION

## When I breathe fire, I am ready to create.

Switch sides and practice the dragon with your left foot forward as you balance on your right knee.

Again, hold the pose and breathe in and out five dragon breaths.

# Chameleons
## (Partner Pose)

### FEELING
### FRIENDLINESS

Lie on your tummy, tuck your hands under your shoulders, and face your partner. Lift up slowly at the same time as your partner. Raise your head and smile at your friend. Keep your arms straight while your body is raised.

### AFFIRMATION

Say together,

## We show each other our friendly colors.

As you become a chameleon, breathe in and out five times. Enjoy your friendly feelings.

# Tiger Twist
## (Partner Pose)

## FEELINGS

## TRUST AND COOPERATION

Tiger cubs build strength, agility, and coordination when they play. Let your tiger cub partner help you turn and flex in this modest twist. Sit cross-legged with your knees touching your partner's as you face one another. Wrap your right hand behind your back and reach with your left hand over to your partner's right hand. He or she also will be doing the same thing. Gently tug on your partner's hand and feel yourself twist and flex to the right. Then, change arms and do the opposite twist to the left.

## AFFIRMATION

Say together,

## We cooperate to help our bodies flex and turn.

As you twist like a tiger, breathe in and out five times before changing sides.

# Opossum

## FEELING
## SATISFACTION

Yoga practice should always end with the most important pose of all, the opossum. The opossum plays "dead" so that no one will bother it. To become the opossum, you must lie down and be perfectly still. This pose gives your body a chance to relax and experience the satisfaction of knowing your feelings were released as you practiced strength, balance, and concentration.

Lie down on your back. Stretch out in a comfortable position with your palms face up. Tighten your body by clenching your fists and curling your toes under. Then, wiggle around to loosen every muscle. Close your eyes and let go, relaxing completely.

## AFFIRMATION

I feel satisfied knowing I have helped my body get strong and flexible. I have expressed my feelings in a healthy way.

Breathe and relax for at least five minutes.

# acknowledgments

Special thanks to Jayadeva, instructor, Integral Yoga of Princeton, for evaluating the text.

Thanks also to the five children who posed for this book: Christina Vilarino, Lauren Eng, Cara Marano, Eshaya Draper, and Samuel Wyatt.

For Craig, my inspiration
—M. H.

To my son, Milo
—M. F.

Marshall Cavendish Corporation, 99 White Plains Road, Tarrytown, NY 10591
www.marshallcavendish.us/kids

Library of Congress Cataloging-in-Publication Data

Humphrey, Mary.
 The Kids' yoga book of feelings / by Mary Humphrey ; photographs by Michael Frost ;
illustrations by Janet Hamlin. — 1st ed.
   p. cm.
 Summary: "This book uses yoga to teach kids about feelings and gives instructions on
how to do 20 simple yoga poses that will help children release their feelings in a fun,
healthy way"—Provided by publisher.
 ISBN 978-0-7614-5424-3
 1. Hatha yoga for children—Juvenile literature. 2. Emotions in children—Juvenile
literature. I. Frost, Michael, 1969- II. Hamlin, Janet. III. Title.

RJ133.7.H86 2008
613.7'046083—dc22

2007026625

The text of this book is set in Ulissa Rounded Regular.

The animal drawings by Janet Hamlin were rendered in black acrylic with a brush on smooth bristol board, scanned in, and converted into a color digital file.

Book designer: Kay Petronio
Editor: Margery Cuyler

Printed in Malaysia
First edition
1 3 5 6 4 2

mc Marshall Cavendish Children